THE PATH TO GLORY

by Bill Burrell

Order this book online at www.trafford.com
or email orders@trafford.com

Most Trafford titles are also available at major online book retailers.

Printed in the United States of America.

ISBN: 978-1-4269-9427-2

Library of Congress Control Number: 2011916086

Trafford rev. 09/23/2011

Trafford
PUBLISHING® www.trafford.com

North America & international
toll-free: 1 888 232 4444 (USA & Canada)
phone: 250 383 6864 ♦ fax: 812 355 4082

ACKNOWLEDGEMENTS

Mr. Eric Helgren and Son

The Tom Cairns Family

The Stan Anderson Family

The Bert Josephson Family

Mr. Tim Orr

Mr. Harley Foss

Mr. Steve Dunsden

Mr. Iory Pugh and George

The many Legions I visited and their members

- The author

THE POEM- "THE PATH TO VICTORY"

FROM THE PRAIRIE FARMS AND CITIES

CAME MANY CANADIANS- SOME POOR, SOME PRETTY

THEY FELT BY 'JOINING UP', THEY WOULD SEE A WORDLY LIFE

SO OFF TO EUROPE THEY SAILED TO THEIR UNKNOWN STRIFE.

MEN, WOMEN JOINED SO THEY COULD SERVE THEIR COUNTRY WITH LITTLE FEAR

OVERSEAS, FIGHTING FOR FREEDOM AND LIBERTY.

THEY SAW THEIR COMRADES WOUNDED, PUT TO DEATH,

SCENES SO HORRIFIC IT WOULD TAKE OUR BREATH.

FOUR YEARS ON THE WARFRON, TO GRUESOME FOR MOST TO SEE

THE SURVIVING MEN AND WOMEN HEADED TO THEIR HOME,

TO SEE THEIR FAMILIES AND FRIENDS THEY HAD LOVED AND KNOWN.

THEY TREAD THE PATH OF GLORY TO FINALLY REACH THEIR FARM OR CITY.

OVER FOUR YEARS OF BATTLE, LEAVING WITHOUT PITY.

TO ALL THESE WHO SERVED, TO THEM AND THEIR FAMILIES

WE SAY THANK YOU ON BENDED KNEE,

FOR BRINGING THE PEOPLE OF THE WORLD FREEDOM AND LIBERTY.

WRITTEN BY BILL BURRELL JUNE 2011

PREFACE

The Dirty Thirties was a hard life for these young men and their families from the Prairies and BC. Some of these men, from farms and small towns often had to leave home to find work. They hopped the rails (took the train) to bigger farms in the south and central parts of Manitoba, Saskatchewan, and Alberta. Some picked fruit in the Okanagan Valley of BC.

Now, these boys who hopped the rails, they litterly rode on the top of Box cars to their work destinations. Having little or no money for a train fare, they used this mode of transportation; it was cold on top of those cars and a little dangerous if you didn't hang on! They found work on thrashing crews, general farm labour and picking fruit. With the outbreak of the Second World War, in 1939, many headed to the bigger centers to enlist. To try for acceptance, fibs about their age and health prevailed for 16 and 17 year olds. They read the signs, JOIN THE ARMED FORCES and SEE THE WORLD. And they did.

ABOUT THE AUTHOR

A little about me, Bill Burrell

As a youngster, I spent the first four years of my life in Manitoba. My uncle, Lorne McCallum was in the Royal Canadian Air Force. I remember seeing him in his uniform, I was in awe! It seemed so neat to see uniformed men to a little guy like me. Little did I know, that the uniform signified, in some cases, war? When World War II ended, for VE day, parents, Grandmother, Grandfather, my parents, my aunt and my sister went out to ceremonies at Rivers Airport, of which my uncle was part of. Many planes flew over against the clear blue sky to celebrate. I recall, these planes dropped thousands of colored ping pong balls on the airstrip.

My family and I moved West to Aneroid, SK. In school, if it was a weekday Remembrance Day, we were allowed to view the veterans, marching the two blocks from the church to the Legion Memorial at the Hall. The temperature was sometimes way below zero with a brisk wind blowing. I admired these men, for honouring their fallen comrades on that terrible cold day! I still think of those men and women taking part. As young boys, my friends and I found a part of an airplane. We pretended it was a Lancaster Bomber, with rear and front tail gunners, We had learned about these war planes from the school library. After school I would stop at my Grandfather's. He had a huge World War II book, and if I was quiet (hush yer gab), he let me read and look at the pictures. My interest in the second World War was perked.

From Aneroid, I moved North to Hudson Bay SK where I worked in the Post review newspaper. Later, I worked, in Regina and then moved to Camose, Alta. Four years later I moved to Kelowna. BC then Summerland an then Vancouver, where I now reside.

During my travel to all those palaces, I met many War veterans, at work, on the streets or in their Legions. My story is derived from the War II stories that they had their families told.

Bert Josephson, RCN
Railway engineer
Retred curler-DJ

THE PATH TO VICTORY

INTRODUCTION

This book was written in honour of the Canadian Soldiers who fought for Freedom in the Second World War. Some returned home victorious. Other gave their lives for our freedom. These are some of the stories of some men and women who served in the Canadian Forces.

They tell of their life before the war, during and post war. How soon it was forgotten about the bravery of these men and women as they fought on The Path to Victory. Nowadays, a majority of Canadians are not aware of the freedom we enjoy in our country. Here are some of the stories told to me by the veterans that I was acquainted with.

The Path to Victory begins with the army life of a Canadian soldier, Stanley George Anderson. Stan was raised in St. Laurent, Manitoba, with his siblings. His father ran an Insurance Business while his mother was kept busy feeding and rearing the family. The only school in town was a Roman Catholic School run by the nuns. Stan attended, but would sooner be out helping his Dad and the men catch fish on Lake Winnipeg on the winter ice. By the time he finished school, he like other prairie boys in the Depression, headed out of province to work. Unemployment was high and hard times hit most everyone.

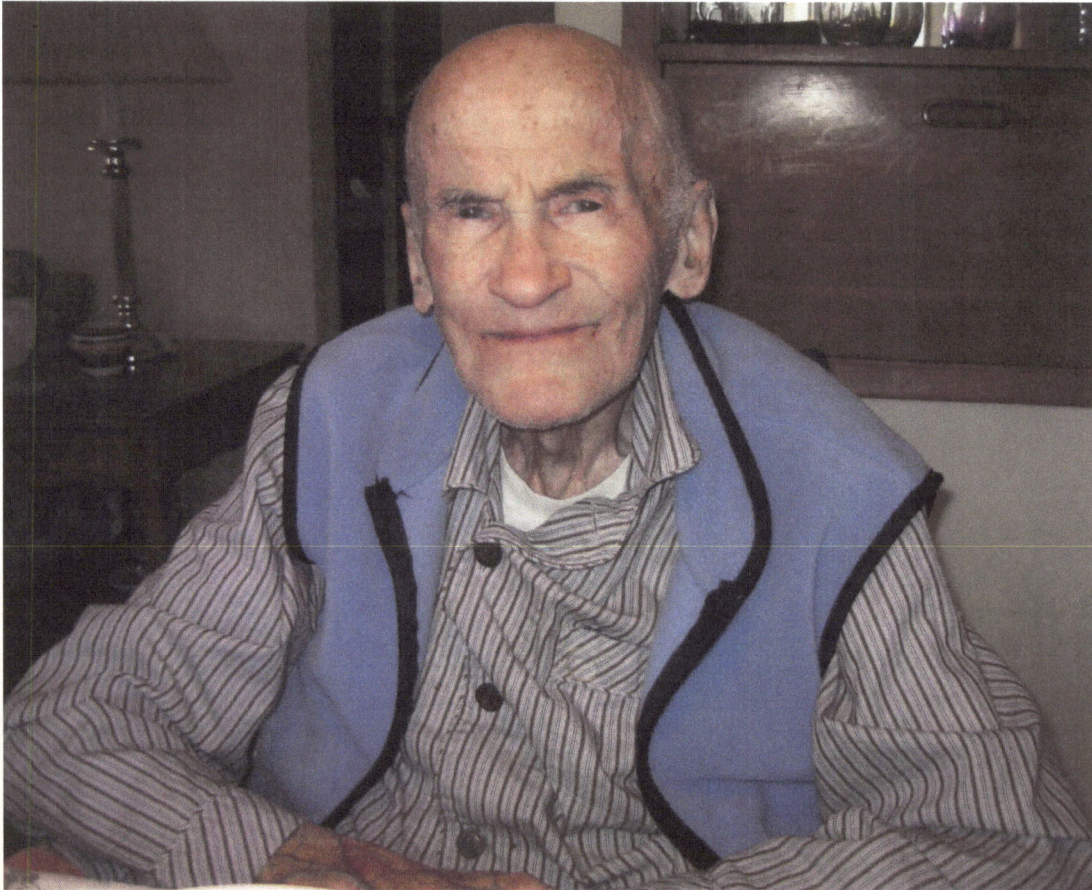

Lt. STAN ANDERSON (1915-2009)

These young men had to find cheap travel to get to the jobs. Stan worked first for his brother at a fishing camp in Northern Alberta. When work ended there he found this cheap mode of travel "Riding the Rails". Unlike riding a comfy passenger train, riding the rails was free. Stan and thousands like him, rode on top of the freight train cars. It was very dangerous for these young free riders with the possibility of slipping while grabbing the car ladders which let to being slammed against the car. The worst scenario was falling off the ladder or the top of the fast moving car.

Stan was on a freight train on the Prairies, chatting with his working buddies, when one mentioned going to the Okanagan in BC, to pick fruit. They arrived in Penticton, via Chute Lake. They felt the police might catch them if they rode through the town. He said they caught a freight on the outskirts of Penticton. As

Stan grabbed the ladder of the car, his one hand slipped and he swung into the car's path hitting his ribs on the side of the car. He managed to hang on and went for a short ride. All the boys were heading to cam set up on Shaha Lake. The big campfire was a welcoming site. Stan set up camp and had some tea they had brewing. He was given some bannock, a type of bread the natives made and he had a restless night with his rib problems. As the sun shone down on the camp, the boys told the injured Stan to go to a doctor in the city. He went to the doctor who said he had badly bruised ribs so he taped him up and the good doctor also gave him a few pills and some vouchers for food. The young man marched back to the camp, feeling much better and to his friends he was well accepted with the food he brought!

The boys from the Prairies picked fruit until the last apple was in the bin in late September. Stan then headed to Saskatchewan. He found work on a small farm near Biggar, SK. Stan was now 26 years of age was a good worker, but had not found a real steady job.

As he arrived in the town, an elderly farmer asked the men who could thresh with him. Stan was the only one and so he threw his pack in the farmer's old truck and off to the farm. The old farmer and the young helper worked side by side until the sunset at 7pm. They went back to the farmhouse where the farmer's wife put out quite a spread. Stan was famished, finishing his big meal he looked to see the old couple fast asleep at the table. It was while Stan worked at the farm, he was told that Canada had declared war on Germany and the forces were asking for recruits, "join and see the world".

Stan headed into Saskatoon where he was accepted as member of the Saskatoon Light Infantry.

OFF TO WAR

Our young soldier set off for home to say his goodbyes and pick up a few belongings. His parents, he said, did not want him to go. There was no stopping him and soon he was back in Saskatoon. The army held their training and lodging at the Exhibition Grounds. It was a short and intensive training program. Stan remarked that they got their uniforms two days before the training ended. All the recruits, part of the nearly 16,000 headed to waiting ships in Halifax. Stan said it was a little crowded but at least they all had a seat. Like clockwork, the train pulled onto a siding at precisely 12 noon.

Stan said for every meal, the same procedure. The soldiers filed off the train, white suited workers followed with tables, white linen tablecloths, cutlery and steaming hot meals. The best meals the soldiers would eat in a long while.

In December, under the 1ˢᵗ Division, they sailed for England, which was at risk of a German attack. I believe he said they sailed in a fleet with their ship, the Almazra. They lived in crowded quarters on board. They spent Christmas on the way to Europe. He said the festive meal was not good but was very grateful that the families back home sent most of the boys treats like Christmas plum pudding. They landed in Liverpool, where Stan and Company spent a few days.

A train was setup and the boys headed to London. The boys were put up in large homes of good citizens of London. Stan said the homes were empty and he felt the British Government found homes elsewhere for the families that gave up their homes for the soldiers. Stan and company trained in Aldershot.

Nearly 2000 officers and over 24,000 men made up the 1ˢᵗ Canadian Infantry Division. From December 1939, Stan waited with the other Canadians. It was felt they were the only Division that had a higher birth rate than rate of death. Some, who joined at the age of 20 (Stan was 26), and they were fathers while waiting in Britain.

Stan and buddy went to London on weekend leave. He said they partied a bit, saw the sights and looked for English ladies. They went to the zoo, where they saw a young lady he admired. She gave him directions and seemed to disappear. Inside, he was delighted, that she appeared again. This young woman was Dorothy Harmon, he soon found out. He later joked to all of us that she was "chasing" him, he wished.

They made arrangements to meet again. After a few dates, she asked him to dinner at her home. The young Canadian soldier in uniform, showed up at the Harmon home. He met Dorothy's parents and her brother, Stan. I believe Stan gained approval with his visit.

Stan and some his fellow soldiers were sent for two weeks to Scotland. The Germans began to bomb London at this time. Stan was worried for the safety of Dorothy and her family. She told hm the authorities had asked residents to go to the bomb shelters set up for them. She felt they would be going there, soon.

Upon Stan's return, he noticed that many more sections of London had been destroyed by German bombs. He set off to the Harmon neighborhood, wading through rubble. When he reached the Street where the house was situated, he was in shock. The house was gone, the street was gone and so was the whole block. He said he thought the worst thoughts, thinking the Harmons were… gone! As he walked the bombed out area, he remembered what Dorothy said to him of the Bomb Shelter. Maybe, he thought, they were there? He stopped an official, and asked him where residents would go for shelter, and headed off with the information.

Of note, Stan told me this story while we were having refreshments at the Fraser and 49th Legion. When he came to the part where he saw the bombed neighborhood, I looked at him, he was silent and tears came to his eyes. What a sight for him to see.

Dorothy tells her version of the story, later in the book, The Dorothys.

Anyway, news got much better as he reached the Shelter and they advised him that, indeed, the Harmon family, were safely inside. He was so happy to see them.

Mr. and Mrs. Stan Anderson
London, England, 1943

The waiting game the Canadians were playing came to an end. The Canadian contingent of 26,000 strong was shipped to Sicily. The young men waded ashore on July 10, 1943, Stan included.

Unknown to Stan, there were many armed forces who joined him as they also landed in Sicily. They included famous Vancouver writer Farley Mowat, Vancouver lawyer and famous city councilor, Harry Rankin, Also joining up with these Seaforth Highlanders was a personal friend of mine, Tom Cairns of Summerland. We will meet up with him later in the book.

The island of Sicily fell in 38 days. Stan was hospitalized soon after the Sicily landing. He had a bad case of tonsolitis and was placed on a hospital ship. He missed the 120 mile march, the short, fierce battles with the Germans and the Italian forces. The Canadians received 2,300 injuries and 562 deaths.

While Stan recovered from his throat infection on the Red Cross ship, he noted these observations. The ship cruised passed the islands of Gibraltar and Malta. Night travel found the lights off on the European side and lit on the African side. Before the invasion by the Canadian Forces on Italy on September 03, 1943.

STAN AT WAR ALONG WITH MANY CANADIAN FORCES

Of the many men and women who I met or knew through
    friends, we now follow their Path. From the Canadian
    Hussars in Aneroid, SK, along with other armed services they were in.
Gordon Manning, Ernie Boyce, Cleve Jacobs, Jim and Ken
    Holland, Jack McCavoy, Sid Middlemost, Frank Carey
Don Schroeder, Don Coleman, Gerald Walls, Vern Gorril,
    Jim and Bob Hardement, Hilton, Gordon, Max and Wilbur
    Eddy, Stan Corbin. These men served in the Canadian
    forces in Europe, other than Sicily or Italy.
    Some of them receive distinguish service awards. More
    will be told of them further in the book.

I recently met Tim Orr, Vancouver. He told of his father Robert James Orr, who served with the Royal Regina Rifles. He spent time in Europe and his battalion was called the johns because so many of them came from farms, thus "farmer Johns". Their battle cry became "Up the Johns!" Robert became Lieutenant Colonel and he and his brave comrades continued into Germany until the end of the War.

When Stan rejoined his troops, a Seaforth Highlander, Tom Cairns was in the same Division. Tom, a strapping young farmer, had joined at the Vancouver barracks on Burrard St. Tom's unit left after Stan's but they both ended up on the Italian front. They and the Eighth Army crossed the Straits of Messina, landing in Italy. Other Canadian Seaforths including the War Hero, Bud Smith, Harley Mowat and Harry Rankin. Both of these men were said to be farmers before joining up.

UP THE BOOT

In the fall of 1943, the Eight Army, with Canadian troops within, marched up the Eastern Coast of Italy. The American 5th Army headed up north up the Western coast. Stan and his comrades encountered hot pockets of Germans who advanced to meet the invading Eight Army. From meeting the Apennine Mountains and further up, fierce fighting took place. Here was my friend Tom battling the Germans alongside his Seaforth buddies, near when Stan was fighting the Germans.

Tom was a strapping young prairie man when he enlisted in the Seaforth Highlanders Armoury just before the bridge on Burrard Avenue in Vancouver. Just 10 blocks from where I now reside. Tom and the Seaforths followed Stan's contingent in a few months time. Tom fought, fierce battles with the Germans. The Seaforth Battle cry rang out "Tuloch Arde" (The High Hill) as the Eighth Army headed to Oratona. I believe Tom stated he was captured near the town of Oratona. There had been fierce fighting between the Germans and the Seaforth Highlanders, lives were lost some of the Seaforths were captured.

TOM CAIRNS AND HIS MARCH TO PRISON CAMP

Tom said the Germans marched the Canadian prisoners North, Tom figured it was just behind the German front soldiers march them to the camp. The Canadian soldiers decided they would not march… they ran. They jogged for about 5 miles and finally the Germans ordered them to halt. Tom said the Germans were doubled over, panting and quite out of breath. When they finally marched (ran) to the farm that served as a camp, the German set up tents for the prisoners and for the German soldier guards and the Canadian prisoners.

When they were assigned their beds, they had a meal at one tent. Up at dawn the next morning the Canucks were put to work on the farm. The Germans were unaware that half their prisoners were farm boys. Tom said the Germans observed their prisoners all day and were surprised no fatigue was shown by their captives. The Germans had lunch and most retired after a day like that.

Tom said one evening he and some friends were gathered in this huge meeting tent. All of a sudden, into the tent came a German officer and a few soldiers. Amongst them was a pretty, petite lady, arms tied behind her back. The officer spoke German gruffly to her. As he stared at her, he swung full force, backhandings her in the face. The officer was outraged , turns and left with his contingent. The girl lay on the tent floor and Tom, being the gentleman that he was, scooped up the injured young lady and put her on one their cots. Tom secured a wet cloth to clean her pretty face. Apparently she was a lady of the night for the German soldiers. She fell out of favour with one officer and he struck her.

My friend Tom was a POW until war's end. After war, Tom married and had two daughters and one son. He farmed south of Summerland, moved to town and worked at Brenda Mines, Peachland. He worked at the tailings dam for many years. His job there ended and he was sent to the mill to work. I was a Secondary Crusher Operator and we operators had one or two helpers to keep the "muck flowing". Tom was an exceptional worker; he outworked all the other helpers. I was proud to have him as a helper.

After the Mine closed in 1990, Tom retired and we lived about 3 block from each other. That is when Tom told the army stories. One day he asked Diane and me "Did your Dad (Stan) remember Mt. Casino?" We answered "Yes". He indicated he wished he had been there, instead of a prisoner of war.

Tom seemed to have a successful and fulfilling life. His sense of humour and kindness to others was his Path to Glory. He passed away in 2008. God Bless!

THE DIVISION AND STAN

WINTER of 1943

As Stan and the allies headed up the Adriatic Coast, they met stiff opposition. The Germans were putting up a front and the weather was bad. Stan said it snowed, rained, thawed and then froze. Machines and men came to a standstill. Men were subject to frostbite and were pinned down as they tried to advance on the retreating Germans. The allies had two lines to breakdown, The Hitler and the Gustav. The battle cry of the Seaforth Highlanders could be heard "Tuloch Ard" meaning high hill, as the Seaforths rallied their men. The Moro was running high and with the German snipers, Stan said the going was tough. On December 6, the river was crossed and now they faced the Moro River Gully. From December 11-18 Stan and company battled in the snow and mud along the Oratona Road, reaching Casa Barardi in the rain on December 13.

Stan said the maps were poor and the Germans were setting up death traps. He went up ahead with the rescue crew. As they came over a hill, Stan saw bodies everywhere! He saw some of his comrades who lost their lives on this field the night before. The stench of death and cordite turned their stomachs as the rescuers searched for the wounded.

Canadian Soldiers at the Moro River Cemetary

They reached the outskirts of Oratona on December 11. The German Elite Paratroopers were there to greet them with continual barrages. Stan said the Germans had mines planted in the vacant homes, under the streets and in the rubble piled up on street corners making it very hazardous to walk the streets.

Fighting from house to house and hand to hand it was gruesome conflict. On December 25, the Seaforth Highlanders captured the Tampitasa Church. The Canadians got a break and some shelter to enjoy the Christmas treats sent from home. The remaining Germans headed North on December 28, leaving the Canadians to regroup. Stan was made a seargeant and he and other officers did a head count of the troops that were diminished by the battle with Germans and the jaundice and malaria the Canadians suffered as well.

After the Germans moved to the Hitler line, the allies were hot on their tail. Stan related that by May 1944, they were in sight of Mount Cassino. The allies were shooting ducks for the Germans at the castle high up on Mount Cassino. He said by the 23rd of May the enemy fire kept their advance to a minimum. It seemed impossible to him, that they would be able to get to the Germans. The Canadians had already suffered casualties by their own guns. It seems that maps were in error and the gun trajectories were miscalculated. These were things that were not told to the soldiers of the Canadian Army. Stan never could understand how their own gun fire could kill their own troops.

Stan mentioned that in last year of fighting they were pinned down in their foxholes with only radios to pass the time. Stan learned later why the Germans had the song "Lily Marleigh" sent to the ally radios, to distract the Canadian and allied soldiers. He said it did just the opposite, as the Germans sang that song so did the Canadians. It was a top song for both!

As the second Division sealed off the front section of Mount Cassino, the Germans dug deeper into the castle for protection. Unknown to them, a top Canadian squad, the Van Doos along with a company of Polish soldiers devised a way to capture Mount Cassino. They climed up the steep backside of the mountain and with stealth, surprised the Germans. Stan said after a lot of gunfire up there, suddenly it was silent; the Germans surrendered, ran or were killed.

With the Gothic line broken the Canadians fought at Corriano Ridge, the end of the Rimi Line and on to Rome. Stan said some of his comrades did not get to Rome. They were loaded in trucks and were off to Brussels. Stan was among them. He said they were in Italy for 22 months, 85,000 strong Canadians. The farthest North the Canadian Forces went was to the Savio River.

The Belgians were jubilant as the Canadians rolled into Brussels, freeing that country of German occupation. Stan said they were mobbed by men and women alike. The same thing happened in Holland as their patrol rolled into cities and towns they were mobbed by all, who were so happy to see freedom again. He said some women jumped right up on their army vehicles.

The long journey ended in the Germany. What a long trip, what a tremendous battle, the Canadians had found THE PATH TO GLORY.

The Dorothys

The book has centered mostly on the Canadian women and men who fought in Italy in World War II.

We now hear the stories of two English ladies who were present in London during the War. Both from London and both named Dorothy.

Dorothy Cottingham was my neighbour in Summerland, BC in the 1970's and 1980's. She was born and raised in London. Upon graduation from school in the late 30's. She was trained to work as an office secretary. Dorothy enjoyed her work and good times with her co-workers, when she heard of work in Germany with better pay. So, off she went to Germany. She was very alert and overheard people saying that a war was eminent. She was also told that the British Government was advising out of country (Germany) workers to return to London. She packed her bag and was home the next day.

Wanting to serve her country in the War, she joined the underground Command Center for the British Forces. Her work involved monitoring the movements of the German Forces. She found working there until wars end gave her character for work after the war. As a good neighbour, her character and charisma showed through.

Dorothy would come over to baby-sit our two children, Jodie and Scott. She related how she was putting them to bed, and as 4 and 6 yr. olds, they told her they must brush their teeth before bedtime, 'Mum said so'.

It was a warm Okanagan morning, Dorene (Mom) was at work; Jodie was in school and Scott and I were out working in the yard. I asked him to stick around, but he and his youth size 4 cowboy boots tended to wander. I searched the yard and all around, even in the house. Where did that boy go? I took a hunch that he was next door. As I approached the Cottingham residence, I spotted those little cowboys boots on the deck. I looked in the Patio Door window to a tranquil scene. Sesame Street was on the big TV, a boy in a big easy chair, cookies and milk at a side table, he had it made!

Dorothy would sometimes come downtown Summerland with us. We had a Volkswagen Rabbit, quite small but with the children and Dorothy in the back and us in the front, lots of room. We had preached to the kids to use their seatbelts! Dorothy was coming for a ride one day and as Jodie and Scott piled in, Dorothy watched. It was her turn to get in she asked Scott to shove over on the seat. He said ' I can't, my seatbelt is fastened and Dad said I had to wear it.' She seemed puzzled but I interjected that there was a middle seatbelt he could use. Problem solved!

Her time served for her country in the War seemed to strengthen her and she was so cool. One day she brought over a wood frame, tube radio, a Stromberg-Carlson. It had fine reception and I use it to this day. Thank you, Dorothy.

She passed away in the valley she loved, perhaps her path to glory, the Okanagan Valley of British Columbia.

The other Dorothy

Dorothy Harmon resided and worked in London when the Germans began bombing London. Dorothy met a Canadian soldier, Stan Anderson, as she was out for a walk. Stan kidded afterward that this London lass was 'chasing him.

They soon were dating and she brought him home to meet the folks. While they were dating, the evening bombing filled the air, whoosh, boom! She said they became used to the bombs such as the doodlebug bomb.

Dorothy's family were advised to find shelter in one of three local bomb shelters. They chose the closest one, an old machine shop. While coming home from work, Dorothy heard a swooshing sound like that of a bomb being dropped. She was told that sound was flares the Germans were dropping so they could view their targets.

She said only transportation failures prevented her and all the other workers from going to work. She said it was the tremendous British Spirit that then Prime Minister, the great Winston Churchill spoke of. The family spent the night there as heavy bombing took place. In the morning, when Stan returned from training that morning he found the house, street and block bombed to rubble. A British Official informed Stan that he could reach the family at the Shelter, which he did.

Stan and Dorothy were married in London, November, 1943. Soon after they had a son, Floyd. After the war, in 1945, Dorothy and son, along with many other War brides were directed to an awaiting ship, The Scythia and with escort ships, sailed across the Atlantic to Halifax. They then boarded trains, Dorothy and Floyd went to Ottawa. There, Stan's cousin, Beth accompanied them to Stan's parents in St Laurent, Manitoba.

Dorothy and family reside in Vancouver.

I thank both Dorothys for their stories. Life in those terrible War Years!

The Royal Canadian Legion

After the Second World War, soldiers, with new brides headed to their home town or city.

They needed a place to gather with friends to wine, dine and dance. Thus, Royal Canadian Legions sprang up across the country. My recollection of first seeing a, 'Legion' was in Aneroid, Sk. During the war the 14th Canadian Hussars set up an armoury to train new recruits.

After the war, it was turned over to the town and veterans for a place to hold community events. I recall us young bucks peeking in at a dance and wishing we were old enough to join in. They held Rembrance parades there until the new Legion Hall was built in the 1950's.

As the stopping spot to lay the wreaths, the hall was an eating place where the Royal Canadian Legion Auxiliary, for the hungry marchers.

The community, as a whole held different events there as well, we students had a few school parties there, too.

A special effort was made by Harley Foss and others to make a real memorial to all who fought for freedom.

With many pictures and war medals, it is a place to be proud of.

After leaving Aneroid at the age of nineteen, I followed R.L. Greenwood to Naicam, Sk. I then moved on to work for Al Mazur in Hudson Bay, Sk. It was the first town I was in, that in 1961 had its own Legion. I went there a few times with my workmate, Ron Brooks. In the spring, the Royal Canadian Legion had an ice bonspiel. I curled with Ron, his wife and Sandra Beggs. Sandra's father had fought in the Second World War.

My next move was to Camrose, Alta., where Branch #57 was very active. They had a number of events including dances and as a printer; I sometimes got free tickets for doing the Legion printing. We had great fun and the live bands made a very good show.

My next branch was in Kelowna, BC. Branch #26 where my cousin Shirley and her husband, Frank and I stopped in a few times.

I moved to Summerland in 1974, I frequented Branch # 22, there. Rembrance Day there was well attended. The march to the Rembrance Cenotaph where wreaths were laid for the lost soldiers. The large group, including the RCMP, then marched to the Legion Hall. Diane, my partner worked for the RCMP so we attended the dinners with the vets and their wives and the RCMP members and their ladies.

Branch #22 was unique in that they had a member who became the head of the Canadian Command; that being Mr. Steve Dunsdon.

Steve not only served in the army during the War, he, as president of the local branch, was very active in organizing the annual two day curling bonsiel in Summerland.

Branch #22 had meat draws every Saturday. My friend, George Pugh, whose father, Iory, fought in the Second World War, and I sat in on many draws.

And we won many, too. After the draw the Ladies Auxiliary served a baron of beef dinner. Saturday nights saw canned music, live bands, karaoke, name that tune, something different every time. Another veteran who helped out at the branch was Bert Josephson. He was a great worker for the annual spiels.

Moving to Vancouver, we went to the Legion on Broadway West, #16 on 49th Ave. E. and Unit 298, Army, Navy & Air force Veterans Club on Main Street, Vancouver.

Stan and I used to walk and talk for 10 blocks to sit in that Legion before his passing. One day they had a 50-50 fundraiser draw. We both bought a ticket. They asked Stan, as a vet, to make the draw. He did and you guessed it, he drew my name for $50. I was also at the #16 branch for the rally for Zone #4, in the Senior Summer Games which were hosted by Prince George, BC

The Main Street Army, Navy & Airforce Unit 298 is one of the most active Legions in Vancouver. We played pool, shuffle board and danced at this place. They had the nicest New Years anywhere. First come first served and with the live band and the party favours, it is excellent. Oh, yes, the admission was free!

The Legions in the cities and the towns where I lived in Western Canada were all integral parts of the communities that they were in. Stan and Dorothy belonged to Branch that used to be on Main Street, north of the present Unit 298. Besides being a place for War Veterans, their families and the general public to go to, The Legion was a generous sponsor for many worthwhile community projects. From school and university scholarships, children's sports, arts and theatre and many more endeavors, including housing for the Veterans.

We can be thankful for the veterans fighting and giving their lives for our freedom, the establishing of Royal Canadian Legions across Canada which have aided all citizens with their support of all their activities. What very great people World War 2 veterans were and are!'

Club Unit 298-23 rd Av and Main Street, Vancouver

Veterans who I knew or heard of:

Frank Carey

Don Schroeder

Don Coleman

Gerald Walls

Vern Gorrill- farmer

Bob & Jim Hardement- farmers

Jim & Ken Holland- farmers

Alf Jordison CPR- worker

Hugh McDowell- store owner

Gordon Manning- owner Aneroid News Magnet newspaper

Ernie Boyce- farmer

Clive Jacobs- Postmaster

Art Wright-farmer

Corbins- Cecil, Sidney-store owner, Eric-barber

Eddys- Hilton, Max- farmers

Lock Brooks- train engineer

Edward Edwards- drug store owner

Wilf Knecht- garage owner

Al Lynch

Sid Middlemiss- farmer

Jack McAvoy- teacher

Leo Olmstead- fuel delivery

Frank Schroeder

Arnold & Raymond Bjore- farmers

My cousin, Mark Burrell was a paratrooper for Canada in the Korean War. After the war he worked for a short time before he contacted Polio (maybe through the war?)

He is confined to a wheel chair and built a fishing boat from his chair. He and his family live in Swift Current where Mark keeps busy with different jobs.

Terrence McCoy- Joined the Canadian Forces in the early 70's and was posted in Germany. He was changing a tire when struck by a car and killed. Terry and I were good friends and he left us early in life.

These people were a steady and influential guidance to all

such as myself in the community.

www.ingramcontent.com/pod-product-compliance
Lightning Source LLC
LaVergne TN
LVHW072111070426
835509LV00002B/111